VEGETABLE GARDENING IN CONTAINERS:

HOW TO SUCCESSFULLY GROW HEALTHY ORGANIC VEGETABLES, FRUITS & HERBS IN RAISED BEDS & SMALL URBAN SPACES FOR A THRIVING HOMEMADE GARDEN IN PATIOS & BALCONIES.

BY EDWARD GREEN

© **Copyright 2019 - All rights reserved.**

The content contained within this book may not be reproduced, duplicated or transmitted without direct written permission from the author or the publisher.

Under no circumstances will any blame or legal responsibility be held against the publisher, or author, for any damages, reparation, or monetary loss due to the information contained within this book. Either directly or indirectly.

Legal Notice:

This book is copyright protected. This book is only for personal use. You cannot amend, distribute, sell, use, quote or paraphrase any part, or the content within this book, without the consent of the author or publisher.

Disclaimer Notice:

Please note the information contained within this document is for educational and entertainment purposes only. All effort has been executed to present accurate, up to date, and reliable, complete information. No warranties of any kind are declared or implied. Readers acknowledge that the author is not engaging in the rendering of legal, financial, medical or professional advice. The content within this book has been derived from various sources. Please consult a licensed professional before attempting any techniques outlined in this book.

By reading this document, the reader agrees that under no circumstances is the author responsible for any losses, direct or indirect, which are incurred as a result of the use of information contained within this document, including, but not limited to, — errors, omissions, or inaccuracies.

Table of Contents

Introduction 1

Chapter 1. Benefits from Container Gardening 4

Chapter 2. Why You Should Grow Organic 10

Chapter 3. Container Gardening.. 15

Chapter 4. Creating the Best Environment for Your Container Plants   21

Chapter 5. Choosing Plants 28

Chapter 6. How to Grow Any Plant... 38

Chapter 7. Growing Herbs 45

Chapter 8. How to Protect Your Plants................................... 50

Chapter 9. Ideas to Make Beautiful Gardening Containers

Chapter 10. Tips and Tricks for Container Gardening 63

Chapter 11. Preparing Your Tools and Supplies 70

Chapter 12. Tips for Starting Seeds 74

Chapter 13. Harvesting and Storing Your Crop...................... 80

Chapter 14. Drying and Preserving Herbs 85

Chapter 15. Herb Gardening 91

Chapter 16. General Upkeep 99

Conclusion 103

Introduction

Container gardens allow you to make any area brighter and more colorful, even when the space is limited in size. You can enjoy growing plants in places where you thought it might be impossible otherwise. Containers placed in corners, suspended from ceilings, window boxes placed on railings, and even small pots placed on a shelf or bookcase are just a few examples for these types of gardens and arrangements.

If you cannot grow a vegetable garden outside of your home because of poor soil, if you are living in a limited space without access to an outdoor patio, or if you only have a small deck, you can still enjoy the simple pleasures that vegetable container gardening offers.

The increasing popularity of container gardens in different parts of the world has taught many people the benefits of cultivating these masterpieces. You might see plants growing in containers on balconies or rooftops, in office spaces, restaurants, and more. People can create special gardens—regardless of the location or the area available to them. Additionally, individuals find they can grow special plants that may require extra attention concerning soil and water—plants they could not manage if they were part of a large garden.

Vegetables and flowers can take on an entirely new look when displayed in a container that highlights their unique shape, size, color, and texture. It offers instant color to a room any time of day, and beautiful displays of plants can often change the entire look of a space. These are some of the reasons why container gardening has become a favorite option incorporated by interior designers when dealing with areas.

Even if you have enough room in your garden outside for planting, container gardens allow you to tailor your decorations around seasonal changes. For example, if you live in a climate that experiences all four seasons, the winter may deem it necessary to move your containers inside where your plants can be protected. The portability of gardens in containers gives you the option of enjoying your foliage year round—even in an area where the weather changes dramatically.

Vegetable Container Gardening offers the option of allowing you to own a garden. It gives you the flexibility to reorder or move your plants around whenever and wherever you like. You also have the freedom to choose the plants you want to grow, whether they are flowers, vegetables, herbs, or combinations of all three. You can even grow tropical plants during the winter months if you keep the plants inside your home. Then, when the summertime comes, you can either transplant your plants outside or simply move the containers outdoors.

Creating a Vegetable container garden makes it possible for those who live in the city to enjoy eating fresh salads with the lettuce, tomatoes, and herbs they have grown. High-rise patios and porches become even more beautiful with the addition of container gardens displaying their arrays of brilliant colors and shapes.

Vegetable gardening in Containers is extremely versatile, is not difficult to achieve, and has many advantages.

Benefits from Container Gardening

Many people consider gardening in a container for several reasons. It is a desirable method of planting compared to the traditional gardening system where tilling is required. Gardeners often complain of back pain, among other health issues, as a result of too much hard work done while gardening. Container gardening offers a concept that does reduce not only the chances of having these health issues but also gives room for you to explore your creativity while planting. Here are some of the several benefits you will enjoy while growing plants in a container:

1. Know Your Food

When root tubers like carrots, potatoes, and radishes are planted, they can be easily harvested by overturning the container on a plastic sheet. It is a more comfortable and accident-free way of collecting these crops. Unlike digging them up where there is the possibility of causing damage to the plants in the process. With container gardening, harvesting has never been safer and more comfortable. Collection in container gardening is quite easy and makes the whole system more interesting.

2. Recycled Material for the Containers

Less Need for Resources

The amount of water and nutrients needed to grow plants in container successfully is less compared to traditional outdoor gardening. Growing plants in the ground requires more water and nutrient because of a larger surface area which makes the water not only spread but also susceptible to evaporation. It is not the case in the container as evaporation is minimal and therefore makes the plants require less watering. It also goes for the nutrients needed by the plants. The box requires less fertilizer application, unlike outside gardening, as long as the right size of a pot is used in growing the plants.

3. The Garden Can Be Moved If You Move To another Apartment

The Benefit of Moving the Container Around

Another advantage of this system of gardening is that it allows you to move the pot to a more suitable location. If you do not want to keep bending to the ground to attend to your plant, you can always adjust the height of your garden to suit you. If you need to move your containers to a better area from more exposure to sunlight, you can easily do so with boxes. It is a benefit that cannot be enjoyed in traditional ground farming.

You Can Grow Plants Indoor

The ability to move a container makes it easy to transfer the pots indoor. It could be either to protect them from adverse weather conditions or to give the home interior an appealing sight. Whatever the reason is, plants growing in containers can do well indoors as much as they do outdoors. Everyone knows sunlight is essential to the growth of plants, but several plants require little sunshine, and they will thrive more quickly indoors. A provision could also be made for artificial light for plants that need more light exposure than they get from the reflection of the sun. For plants to thrive indoors, the right conditions must be put in place, such as keeping the containers near a window to enjoy the reflection of the sun or supplying artificial lights. It is a significant advantage for those who are mobility-challenged or too old to work under the sun as they can enjoy what they love doing within the comfort of their home.

The versatility, accessibility, mobility, and flexibility of growing plants in the container are some of the great reasons why it is the right choice for you. You do not have to worry about your garden whenever you change the environment and move to another location. Your container can also move with you to your new home. You have the opportunity to vary your garden's color scheme and give your outdoor the attractive display you want. Container gardening doesn't require much garden tools and equipment. You can always use what you have at home and start creating your garden according to your budget, no matter how low it is.

Easier Pests and Diseases Control

The control of pests and disease is a major concern in gardening generally, especially in-ground traditional gardening. Failure to control pests and conditions will result in poor harvest or complete loss of the affected plants. The risk of this is, however, very minimal in container gardening as the effect of pests can easily be noticed and hence, controlled before it becomes a major problem. Pests and disease control in container gardening usually require little or no chemical application. It makes the harvest almost always chemical-free. In dealing with the pests, cotton buds soaked in rubbing alcohol can be used to eliminate pests like aphids, while brush can be used to remove larger insects.

The Growth of Weed Is Limited In Container Gardening

One of the disadvantages of traditional gardening is, having to put up with the weeds. It is very limited in the container if at all, it is experienced. It can also be quickly addressed without having to use toxic chemicals, which could affect the growing plants. Container gardening is, therefore, a suitable method not just for experienced gardeners but also for those with little or no experience.

The Luxury of Time and Convenience

One of the major attractions of this concept of gardening is the convenience that comes with it. It is such a secure system of farming that the elderly or those who cannot go out can adopt indoor. Unlike traditional gardening, gardening in containers gives you the luxury of time as the weather or general environmental condition does not limit them. You do not have to wait for a particular planting season before growing a specific plant. Container gardening makes it possible to grow plants anytime and anywhere as long as the right growing condition is met within the pot. Its method of gardening makes gardening an acceptable practice for everyone and anyone, regardless of how occupied they are.

The Benefit of Choosing Your Growing Medium and Creating Your Growing Condition

In container gardening, you have the opportunity to try out different types of growing mediums to get the best yield possible. Some of the growing medium you could use includes; soil, expanded clay pellets, coco coir, and peat moss. Its system of gardening allows you to create the best growing condition for your plants. You have the option of purchasing soilless potting mixes or create the increasing status of your plants. You can adjust the light, the soil pH, and nutrients to suit what the plants need for maximum yield.

The Benefit of No-till Gardening

The container provides an easier way to grow plants without having to till the ground. Anyone who has ever had to cultivate the field knows how much of hard work it is. In addition to developing being a strenuous exercise, recent studies have shown that tilling the soil affects some natural organisms which are required for the growth of the plants. It makes the concept of container gardening appreciable as it provides the opportunity of creating a suitable growing condition such that the maximum result possible is obtained without digging the ground. Container gardening helps you to save time and energy because it is a no-till kind of gardening.

A Great Solution to the Issue of Limited Space

The availability or non-availability of space is never an issue when gardening in a container. It is because this method does not require a filed or vast farmland before it can be practiced. You do not need a ground. You can have your plants growing perfectly on a window sill, or a balcony, or anywhere suitable. The maximum utilization of space is one of the top benefits of container gardening.

Why You Should Grow Organic

Today though, more gardeners are tending towards the organic path, yet there are times when non-organic gardening is necessary.

You will know from your grocery shopping that there is a difference between organic and non-organic produce, which is often reflected in the price. There is a fairly significant difference in the two approaches for the container gardener. However, you will find that organic products tend to have a better flavor.

You shouldn't feel you are pushed into organic gardening because it is "the thing to do" and should take an approach that suits you. Most gardeners tend to be mostly organic but with the occasional non-organic method thrown in.

You're growing organic when you grow plants without using chemicals for pest or weed control or fertilization. If you want your plants to be 100% organic, you can buy organic seeds and organic soil too, even though many gardeners don't go that far and will buy regular seeds and soils but opt for natural methods of caring for their plants.

Benefits of Organic Food and Gardening

The advantage of organic gardening is that it is environmentally friendly, so you are not introducing artificial and potentially dangerous chemicals into the soil. Organic fertilizer, for example, will not cause any harm to the environment and improves the quality of your land, whereas chemical fertilizers cause runoff that gets into the water system, plus they only provide a temporary boost of nutrients.

According to numerous studies, it appears that organic vegetables contain higher levels of nutrients than their non-organic counterparts. According to a 2001 study, organic produce was 27% higher in vitamin C, 29% higher in magnesium, 21% higher in iron, and 14% higher in phosphorous.

Perhaps one of the biggest advantages of organic gardening is that it is cheaper than non-organic gardening, and yet you will get a product that is more expensive when bought directly from a store. The store-bought fertilizers can be costly, yet you can make your organic fertilizers for virtually nothing!Comfrey tea, horse manure and compost can all be made from few ingredients, they are natural and they're great for your plants too.In addition, you can also integrate the companion planting method and encourage beneficial insects to your garden to help keep pests away and avoid any chemical.

The downside of organic gardening is that it is considered a harder work because many of the methods used are more time-consuming. For example, you don't use sprays to keep weeds down but pull them up by hand.You will have to learn how to do some more planning, such as for crop rotation and companion planting. Still, for me, the results are much more rewarding and the vegetables far tastier.

Also, keep in mind that you are going to plant more densely than you would in the soil. If anything with organic gardening, you get a higher yield in the smaller area because you are not dowsing your plants with potentially harmful chemicals, and you have a highly nutritious soil.

GMO (Toxic Chemicals) and Why You Should Avoid Them

Many pesticides are linked to cancer, congenital disabilities and nerve damage. In a smaller area such as a container garden, the effects are likely to be much more concentrated.Certainly, in containers, I would be as close to organic as I could not only for this reason but also because containers can be indoors or nearer to your home and so the chemicals will linger in the atmosphere.As time goes by, scientists are finding more and more health risks associated with the use of chemicals on food.

A few years ago, chemical DDT was considered safe to use on food. It was used as a pesticide and after years of use, it was discovered that this chemical was highly toxic, remained in the food and water and was causing serious illness in people.

My recommendation to you is to be as organic as you can.Avoid chemical sprays and toxic chemicals, but if you need to use sprays for anything, then look for organic ones, there are plenty on the market, which are food safe.It will help avoid the build-up of potentially harmful chemicals in the vegetables you are growing.

There is no right or wrong answer to the question, "Should I grow organically?" but more and more home gardeners are moving this way to reduce their impact on the environment, to protect their health and to grow better-tasting produce.

Container Gardening

You might ask yourself why container gardening when you can plant a garden in the ground.

Why Should You Choose To Grow Your Plants In Containers?

It helps eliminate overcrowding. If you are entertaining, you can arrange the plants in different parts of the home or patio. The colors and foliage can be mixed to create different patterns and effects. Rare and unusual varieties that have special soil and light requirements can more easily care.

Aside from the visual effects of container gardening, there are other reasons, which include yard conditions. If you have ever had problems with termites or moles, container gardening is certainly the key. Having gardens too close to your houses is not a wise move, because the water you use on them seeps down to your foundation and attracts termites. For those of us that have small yards or live in apartments or town-homes, container gardening might be the right choice.

It's a real time saver too!

In areas where there are very hot and dry summers, there can be drought, and potted plants don't require as much water as a full garden planted in the yard. In the North, you can utilize tropical plants. They can be pot and treated as summer specimens and then brought in for the winter. The same plants can remain outdoors all-year-round, where the climate is normally warm and sunny.

How to Plan Your Container Gardening

Planning Your Container Garden

Nothing beats the feeling of getting to use your herbs and vegetables, and even flowers, straight from your garden.

There is a wide variety of plants that can be planted and grown in a container garden. With the right amount of planning, you can easily grow just about any type of plant you choose, given that their living conditions are met, of course.

- Plan which plants to grow. Plants have certain requirements that need to be met for them to grow properly. Therefore, you cannot just plant whichever plant you desire. You have to take into consideration the weather, climate and overall environment of where you live. Make a list of plants you want to grow and check their sun, water and soil requirements.

- Evaluate your house. Before you buy seeds or seedlings, carefully evaluate your home.

Determine the areas which get the most sunlight, count how many hours the sunlight shines on those areas and identify the places which are partially shaded. Once you have listed those down, compare the requirements of the plants that you wish to grow and choose accordingly.

- Determine where to place the plants. If the area in your house which gets the most sun does not have enough space, choose to hang your containers or create shelves to place your plants on. These steps are very important, especially if you plan to expand your indoor garden in the future. You can also choose to set your plants somewhere else and then move them outside to get some sunlight; however, the constant moving may stress them out, which can hinder their growth.

Choosing the Containers: How to Choose the Right Pot for Every Plant

Picking the Right Containers

In truth, there is no specific or right container to use for container gardening. There are so many containers that you can choose to use. You can decide to use pots, old jugs or cartons or even watering cans. But to help you choose among hundreds of choices, here are some guidelines that you can follow.

- Style of the container. There are hundreds or even thousands of container styles. You can choose to use anything that you want at all. You can grow your plant in a clay pot, a fishbowl, in a shoebox or even in a trash can. Your choice will be depending on your budget, your design preference and the type of plant that you wish to grow.
- Size of the container. Of course, the larger the box, the higher the chance that your plants will grow healthy and strong. The advantage of using larger pots is that you need to water less frequently because the more soil there is, the longer the moisture will be held. However, if your space is limited, then you need to consider planting smaller plants that can survive in a limited space.

- Self-watering container. If you frequently travel or want a container garden but do not have that much time to tend to it, you can purchase a self-watering box to make sure that your plants get watered regularly. A self-watering container is very convenient to own. Still, if you live in an area where it mostly rains, you might have to monitor your plants more closely to make sure that they do not drown and die.

- Drainage. As mentioned earlier, you can choose to use any container that you want. Still, you have to make sure that it has holes for drainage, or it is a material that you can easily make holes to.

Creating the Best Environment for Your Container Plants

Where will the container be located?

Light is one of the most important considerations if you want to grow happy, healthy, prolific flowers. Watch the sun and note if the container location is sunny, shady or partly shaded. Be sure to pick flowers that will thrive in that light.

Is this container going to be a centerpiece point or part of a grouping?

If this container is a stand-alone, "look at me" planting, it will need to be a large outstanding container planted with large foliage and flowers.If it's part of a grouping, you will have more leeway in choosing a variety of plants and containers. If you are planning on grouping your containers, apply the "rule of three." An odd number is always more pleasing when grouping anything, whether it's plants or containers.

What feeling am I trying to convey?

What type of home do you have? Is it stately and traditional? Homey and comfortable, a log cabin in the woods, or stucco home in a development?

The containers and flowers you choose should reflect that atmosphere. Look around at various containers in your area. Take photos with your phone while out walking. Look at gardening magazines and take note of the types of vessels and flowers used in areas similar to where you live.

Eventually, you will get a feel for what looks and feels right for you and your environment.

Where and When to Plant

Don't plant too early

Many people, even long time gardeners can plant too soon. Winter is gone, it is officially spring season, and everyone has cabin fever. Gardeners are ready to get out and grow! Make sure you know what zone you live in, and this will tell you when to expect the last frost. For most plants, cold is your enemy. By planting too early a late spring frost will destroy all of your hard work. It can be discouraging to make a great effort and then wake up and look out the window, and see everything covered with frost. Also, see below for a chart of when to grow based on soil conditions and frost times.

Your garden must be in an area that gets a lot of sunlight. Plants need the sun to photosynthesize, so planting away from the sun means slower growth and fewer crop yields. You want to plant where the daylight lasts for the day.

It may seems like common sense, but this is one of the main reasons why farmers do not yield enough crops. You must plan. Know what you want to plant seasons ahead and purchase the necessary seeds and tools to get the harvest started.

You can check online to see when your favorite fruits, veggies, nuts and herbs are in season. Waiting until that season comes to plant may mean that you won't yield the product you could have if you would have planned it before.

Scheduling is the key yet again when it comes to planting in this way. You must have your crops in the rotation when you are prepping for the year.

Organic agriculture reduces the use of non-renewable sources of energy. It means that you won't be wasting as much of the earth's resources by farming. Growing organic lessens the greenhouse effect and global warming, which is a major issue, especially for those of us who live in the northern hemisphere. It is only possible because growing organic stops carbon from seeping into the atmosphere while it's still in the soil. The increased carbon storage raises productivity because crops that are grown in carbon-rich soil tend to increase agriculture against climate change. It means that organic vegetables have a significantly better chance of surviving our rough climate than non-organic crops.

Make sure you choose the right plants for your location. You won't find papayas growing in most organic areas because the climate isn't right. You can learn which plants will thrive in your garden by checking the USDA's Hardiness Zones.

The Different Climatic Conditions across the American States

Over many centuries, plants have adapted to particular environmental conditions. They have grown accustomed to natural light sources and unlimited soil where their roots could spread. They have also been freely moved by wind. As a result, an average indoor environment is naturally hostile to most plants.

Even if a plant grows in a container, not all the natural conditions are present, unless the gardener provides them. Nevertheless, plants are adaptable even in hostile environments. They can struggle to keep living and growing. But, when the situation is close to nature, the plant could quickly respond by flowering and providing fruits and fragrance.

If the gardener provides adequate light, container, and soil, a lot of plants could do well in indoor settings.

Container gardening allows you to control the microenvironment of your garden. Several environmental factors will affect your container garden.

Light

Light and temperature are very important factors that can help you successfully grow plants in containers. The best thing about container gardening is that it offers convenience and portability. If you live in the temperate regions, the light conditions change, so make sure that you move your plants to get enough sunlight and avoid high temperatures.

Wind

The wind is considered a seasonal problem, and if your area suffers from strong winds during the summer, the containers may tumble over, especially if they are small. To prevent the wind from toppling over the pots, combine the weight of the box and soil to the upper portions of the plant for stable support. If your plants are blooming or have big leaves, and there is a strong wind – relocate them.

Heat Absorption

Too much heat can kill your plants. However, it is important to take note that the type of material of your pot can affect the heat absorption of your plant greatly. If you only have dark-colored plants, you can type Mediterranean plants, herbs and succulents that can withstand high heat temperature.

Seasonal Changes

Seasons can affect the growth of your container plants. The best thing about container gardening is that the changes in the season do not have a big impact on the plants as you can relocate your plants to different places in your house where they will be safe.

Choosing Plants

Choosing and growing your vegetables for your container garden is safer and healthier. You can be sure that no pesticide will harm you or your family. It is not hard to grow vegetables in containers as long as you know the right boxes to choose, the soil preparation, and the care and maintenance that you need to do.

For starters, you can try growing beans in a 12-inch wide container.

What to Grow In Your Garden

You can grow beets like a red ace, but make sure not to crowd the beets.Six plants in a 12-inch wide container should be enough.

Carrots have smaller varieties called short 'n sweet, little fingers, and Thumbelina.The smaller types only need six to eight inches deep containers to grow.The longer models may require deeper vessels.

Cauliflower, cabbage, broccoli, Brussels sprouts, kale, and other Cole crops can grow well in containers.They require big enough boxes, and won't grow well if you insist on using small containers.

Eggplant needs a five-gallon container to grow well.You also need to push a stake into the pot to provide proper support for the plant.

Lettuce and greens are the favorites of the most novice gardeners.They are not particular about the size of your container, although it is recommended to give them the proper spacing.Just sprinkle the seeds, keep the soil damp, and soon you will be harvesting fresh produce for your salad.

You can try radishes, cucumbers, spring onions, peppers, peas, squash, and others. You can buy your seedlings from a nursery or seeds from a garden supply shop.

Vegetables that are considered light lovers are beans, eggplant, pepper, and cucumber. Those that are okay with partial light are lettuce, carrot, spinach, broccoli, beets, peas, and collard greens.

Growing vegetables in containers will ensure that you and your family are eating the right kind of healthy food.

Seeds or Seedlings

You must predetermine if you should start planting the seeds outdoors or preparing them indoors in a controlled environment. That will depend on the type of plant you are growing, and the viable months left in your season. There is also the question of whether or not the seedling transplants well.

•Starting from **seeds** work if you are early into the season, and will plant veggies that mature into seedlings rather quickly (i.e., green peas, beans, summer squash, beets, carrots, corn, cucumbers, garlic, lettuce, parsnips, radishes, turnips, and watermelon).

•Cultivating **seedlings** indoors is best for pepper, any herbs, broccoli, Brussels sprouts, cabbage, cauliflower, celery, chard, eggplant, kale, leeks, onions, peppers, and tomatoes. These plants have slow maturation processes and can tolerate the disturbance of their roots during handling and transplanting.

When in doubt, look at the seed packaging and ask your local veggie shop proprietor.

A Special Type of Soil

In most cases, you seed your plants in another nutrient-rich mix of starter soil. You can buy this in small bags, or you can mix your own. The formula is simple, but you still need to buy the raw materials:

•4 parts compost (preferably screened)

- 2 parts coir

- 1 part vermiculite

- 1 part perlite

For best results, mix now, leave alone for a few days, and then plant your seeds. BTW, there is no need to buy those particular types of seedling containers. I personally prefer to use old paper Mache egg trays laid on top of plastic egg trays. This way, even if the paper dissolves, you still have the plastic.

Toughen Up Young Sprouts!

If you are seeding indoors, you want to alter the seedlings to the outdoor environment before transplanting. That means placing the seedlings outdoors under indirect sunlight i.e., north facing. Bring the plants in when it gets too cold or too hot. After a couple of days hardening, the seedlings are good to go!

Easy Vegetables That Practically Grow Themselves

It's only natural. When you first start any project – and small-space gardening is no exception – you'd like to be successful at it. When you excel at something, then you want to keep doing it. So, you obviously would like to excel at your first attempt at growing vegetables, herbs and flowers. You're much more likely to adopt it as your hobby when you perform well.

Before you take a deep breath, thinking "boring!" look at these wonderfully diverse lists of the easiest vegetables to grow.There are more, but these lists will kick-start your thinking.And you're guaranteed to find many of your favorite foods.

1.Radishes

Radishes are easy to grow because they're practically pest-free. That eliminates much of the worry and maintenance that many experience with gardening.You can easily start this plant from seed at the beginning of the growing season and enjoy a zesty addition to your salads in the season.You'll want to choose from CHERRIETTE, Cherry Belle or Scarlet Globe for best results.

2.Carrots

Who can resist carrots?You'll be amazed at your bountiful yield of carrots on your first gardening attempt.Few insects bother them, so they're low maintenance. You'll just want to use soil that isn't very rocky.While it won't affect the taste, rocky soil produces crooked carrots.A carrot is ready to harvest, by the way, as soon as the top breaks through the soil.The easiest varieties to grow are Scarlet Nantes, Danvers Half Long, and Sweet Treat.

3.Lettuce

You may have been told that this was difficult to grow.Don't believe it! It is one of the easiest vegetables for a novice gardener to plant successfully.Once you plant the seed the only thing you need to do is to watch it grow.

Don't limit your selection to merely leaf lettuce.Its vegetable comes in many varieties – all of which are delicious (and healthy!).Spinach is a type of lettuce, as is arugula.You may also want to try cultivating micro-greens. If you've never eaten these, you're in for a treat.They're tender greens that are at perfection when only a few weeks old.

4.Cucumbers

Yes, cucumbers!If you've ever seen these plants in a garden, then you know they're born to sprawl and spread. You only need to ensure that you give them plenty of room for their roots.If you do that, you'll be enjoying the crispness of fresh cucumbers right from your garden. Some of the best types for beginners to grow include Diva, Straight Eight and Salad Bush Hybrid.

5. Tomatoes

All you need for this plant to grow healthy and produce a crop is a good dependable water supply and sunlight. If you can deliver that, then you'll be enjoying tomatoes all summer – and probably sharing them with family and friends too!

Most gardeners don't start tomatoes from seeds but use what are called starter plants.You can buy these at your local nursery – even many home improvement stores carry them.If it's your first time growing tomatoes, try either the Big Boy or Roma variety.

6. Peppers

Peppers, specifically green bell peppers, are great for a beginning small-space gardener.The one fact you should know about it is its craving for warm temperatures.It's a slow grower, so don't be alarmed if it seems to "lag" your other crops in development.It is to be expected.The best time to harvest this vegetable is when the pepper is between three to four inches long and firm.

7. Beans

Think green beans.You even have some choices if you decide to plant this vegetable.Most grains are easy to grow.As a small-space gardener, you may also want to consider broad and pole beans.Broad beans are extremely easy to manage.As for the pole beans, the only issue you'll encounter is the need for a trellis for them to climb.But erecting a trellis is worth the little bit of extra effort if it means enjoying fresh beans.

8. Peas

A member of the legume family, the pea is a sure winner in a small-space garden.Choose from sweet or sugar beans; you can't go wrong with either.Both are nearly maintenance-free.And the only pest they attract is fruit flies.The good news is that these insects are easily controlled organically with NEEM oil.You might have heard of it.It's used by many as a natural repellent against mosquitoes that may be carrying the West Nile Virus.

You can begin planting these early as March, depending on where you live.There are only a few factors you'll want to consider.You'll want to make sure that if your pea plant grows tall, you provide a trellis or even a fence for it.If it's a shorter plant, make sure the container you place it in is deep.Harvest, then enjoy!

9. Onions

Okay, I'll agree; onions are not the most glamorous vegetable you can grow.But it sure can add zing when you put it raw on a hamburger or other sandwich.And it has a delicious sweet taste when SAUTEED. It enhances just about any meal.And if you're growing peppers as well – then you have yourself some fresh SAUTEED combination that can't be beaten.The only factor you need to consider is their love for the water.

How to Grow Any Plant

Now that you have your location, all of your supplies and your choices of fruits and vegetables you wish to grow, it is time to put it all together and start the planting process.

1. Start with the containers. Make a final check to ensure that the insides of each vessel are clean and free of debris. Also, closely inspect them for cracks. You want to find them now before you put them into use. Once you place your soil and plant in them, the increased weight and pressure will find these discrepancies for you.

2. And then, check your soil. It might sound simple, but make sure that you have more than enough for your containers. Leaving plants lying around, even in the shade, while you make a last-minute trip to the store puts them under stress.

3. Check for moisture. Soil needs to have the right consistency of moisture before you use it. While it does not require you to saturate it with water, it does mean is that it needs to contain more moisture than the bone-dry consistency that it presents when it is brought home in the bag. Using soil that is too dry will be hard to balance after planting. The roots will be feverishly searching the ground for any signs of moisture. Waiting until after it is planted will stress the plant.

It will also be much more difficult to balance the moisture level throughout the soil after planting has occurred.

The best approach to moisturizing soil is to place the amount of dirt that you need in a bucket. Add a small amount of water to the ground and mix it until it is sufficiently damp. It means that it contains enough moisture that it is wet. Still, there should not be any patches where the soil is densely packed together because of a high concentration of water. Continue adding a small amount of water to the container until all of the ground is saturated.

4. Prep the plant. If you went with a seedling, your plant would already have a formed ball of soil packed around its root system. You mustn't try to pull this off. Attempting to do so could easily damage the roots and jeopardize the health of the plant.

Your plant's root ball will also probably contain small round pellets. These pellets are fertilizer the grower has used and are not a reason for concern.

To transplant the seedling, you first need to inspect it. Take a good look at the soil surrounding the root ball. If it is rather dry, you will want to add some moisture to it before planting- even if you have moistened your soil in the container.

Place the seedling in a small container of water and allow it to absorb some of the water into the root ball. It doesn't need to float in water, or the soil surrounding the root ball will begin to loosen and break apart.

5. Move the plant. Once the seedling's root ball has received a sufficient amount of water, it can be transplanted into the new container. If the seedling's soil was sufficiently wet, then all that is necessary now is to transplant it from its original box to the new one. Since these seedlings are very delicate, you must take your time when removing them from their old container.

Even though most seedlings will be small, it is common for some people to pull them out of their old containers simply, which is the wrong thing to do. Drawing on the trunk of the seedling will cause it to snap in two or, at the very least, crack the vault of the plant, which could eventually kill it.

The preferred method of removal is to place the seedling's trunk between the second and third fingers of one hand and turn the container upside down. Grasp the bottom of the container with your free hand and gently shake it to loosen the seedling from its container. In some instances, the plant may be lodged in tightly, so it might become necessary to tap the bottom to move it.

The plant may still resist moving from the old container. If this occurs, take a butter knife and slide it around the inside of the vessel on all sides between it and the plant. It should free the seedling.

6. Inspect the root ball. Depending on how long the plant has been allowed to grow in its old container, it may have established quite an elaborate root system. There are times when you remove a plant, and all you will see is a twisted heap of roots with no visible soil. It means that the plant was allowed to remain in its container for far too long. While the plant can still be used, it will need some additional help to get started.

When roots are densely-packed together, you will need to separate and loosen them somewhat to allow them to get a head-start once they are placed in the new container.

If you leave them in a mangled mess, the plant will probably still grow, but it will take longer for the roots to realize that they are no longer constricted in a small place. Helping them speed up the process.

You will want to gently loosen the roots of the seedling by pulling them apart. Stay away from the base of the plant as you can easily pull roots off the plant base, injuring the plant. Pry the roots apart as much as you can and then plant.

If you see that the root ball is densely packed with soil, you can also help this situation by taking your butter knife and making some small incisions in different places in the ground to loosen it up. The marks do not have to be deep, and several small ones are much better for the plant than one or two large ones. Digging into the root ball too deep with a knife can damage roots deep down that you will not be able to see.

7. Plant your plants. Your new container should be filled with soil up to approximately one to one-and-half inches from the outer rim. Take your trowel or even your hand and remove a small amount of soil form the middle. Now, place the plant in the hole and pack the soil back around the plant while holding it upright.

You have to be very careful when packing soil around the plant as several things can happen. First, you may tend to push too hard around the plant in an attempt to seat it in the dirt firmly. In doing so, you can very snap off the plant at the ground or just below it. If you find that the plant isn't firm in the soil, gently remove the land and the plant and dig a slightly larger hole and try again. Never try to force the plant into the ground.

Second, is that you can end up with a plant that is buried too deep. You want the root system to be submerged, but not part of the trunk of the plant. Judge how high the soil needs to cover the plant.

Make sure that the plant is sitting straight so that there is less likely of a chance that it will tip over or grow at an angle. As it begins to produce vegetables, the added weight on one side could jeopardize the stability of the entire plant.

8. Watering. Surprisingly enough, this involves more than just dumping water on the plant. If water isn't distributed evenly, you take the chance that the plant will not receive valuable water in some parts of the soil. Since the plant has already been put under some stress through transplanting, it does not need the added importance of having to search for water, too.

When you water a new plant for the first time, the water is likely to drain through the soil very quickly since it has just been recently moved into the original container and hasn't had sufficient time to become packed. Even if the ground was moistened before the plant was planted, the soil still needs even more water to give the plant the best chance for survival.

If you dump water on the loose soil in the container, chances are very good that the land will become saturated, and the root ball will receive very little of the water. Why would this happen? Because the root ball is denser, and the water will be diverted to flow through the easy and loosing soil instead.

Instead of flooding the plant with a large volume of water all at once, a better approach is to give the plant a slow, steady drink so that it will allow it enough time to seep into every area—including the roots. It can be accomplished in some ways.

To complete your planting, you will probably have to add a little more soil to the container. When water is applied to the plant, it will automatically compact some of the lands on the surface, creating an indentation that needs to be filled. Some people also like to top off the surface surrounding the plant with mulch, sawdust, tree bark particles, landscape fabric or any assortment of other materials. It does not only help to keep precious water from evaporating, but it also serves as a barrier to help discourage the growth of weeds.

It is a good idea to label your plants with tags, so you know what varieties of each plant you are growing.

Growing Herbs

Grow your Herbs in Containers

Herbs can bring out the natural goodness of the food you eat.Most homemakers are not without potted herbs in their kitchen.The good thing about having fresh herbs in your kitchen is that you don't need to rush to a supermarket to get some in case you suddenly run out of your needed grass.

A good selection includes parsley, oregano, sage, rosemary, thyme, mint, basil, and chives.

Since most herbs like water, it is important to supply them with water all the time. However, there are also the so-called Mediterranean herbs that prefer soil that looks almost like sand.Mediterranean herbs include lavender, sage, rosemary, oregano, and thyme.Unlike most herbs, Mediterranean herbs will rot faster if the soil is too damp. You need to use pebbles or sand mulch around the said herbs.

The ideal place for your herbs is the kitchen. Just make sure to give your herbs the things they need most like sunlight and water.

Some herbs such as lemon balm, mints, and lemon verbena are invasive. Keeping them in containers can prevent them from causing trouble for other herbs in the garden.

You can choose to mix the herbs in a planter, but keep the invasive grasses in their respective containers to avoid taking over the space of other herbs.

Don't worry about frequent herb harvesting. Your herbs gain a lot of benefits from it. When you snip the tips off, the rest of the plant is somewhat stimulated to grow faster.

Getting your fresh supply of herbs from your garden most of (if not all) the time is not only cheap but also healthier.

How to Take Care of Your Herb Plants

Essential Care and Maintenance

After planting your preferred fruits, vegetables, and herbs, you need to observe proper maintenance and care. Taking care of your container garden is not difficult. Still, compared to a traditional garden, a container garden needs extra watering and feeding.

Watering

Most plants need frequent watering unless otherwise stated, as in the case of Mediterranean herbs.Potting soil quickly dries out, especially during windy or hot weather.You may need to water your plants more than once a day if the weather becomes unbelievably hot.In some cases, you may need to add liquid fertilizers, and you can use your watering can for that.

To check if your plant needs more water, insert your finger into the soil.If you feel that the land within the first few inches from the top is bone dry, then you need to water your plant.Make sure that your water penetrates the roots of your plant.

Applying Fertilizer

There is a need to fertilize your plants every two weeks to make sure that they get the right amount of nutrients.Liquid fertilizer is the easiest to use because you only need to mix the fertilizer with water and pour it onto the soil down to the roots.Organic fertilizer is a wise choice.

Beware of Pests

Although a container garden is less prone to pests than a traditional garden, there is still a chance that an infestation might happen.If you notice the presence of parasites, act immediately and remove possible sources of the pests.You can also apply NEEM oil on the leaves and stems of your plants to prevent the pests from invading your garden.The oil acts as a natural fungicide and pesticide.It also discourages the feeding of the pests.

Ample Sun Exposure

Plants need sunlight to thrive and grow, so make sure that your plants are getting the required amount of light.In the absence of natural light, you can use your artificial lighting that still makes photosynthesis possible.

Regular Pruning

Make your plants look fresh and alive all the time by pruning them.Dead leaves can make your plant look dull and unappealing, so you need to remove the dead leaves right away.Spray the leaves with water to remove the dust.

Plants with Disease

If you suspect that a certain plant in your garden has a disease, it is best to isolate the said plant and try to cure it.If the condition becomes worse, then it is best to discard the plant as well as its soil. Using the contaminated soil of the dead plant will only cause a problem.

Some Parting Words

It may take a while before you get used to container gardening. You need to exercise patience, diligence, discipline, perseverance, and willingness to learn and discover new things. Your container garden may not look appealing now, but understand that you have just begun. Your passion and your container garden need some time to bloom into something more radiant and beautiful. Be patient so that you will reap your reward.

How to Protect Your Plants

Containers that have once been rich in color and foliage tend to fade and fail, gradually becoming worn out as the midsummer begins to roll in. As the temperatures start to rise, pretty blossoms and fleshy leaves start to wither and disappear. Fortunately, with proper care, your containers can flourish with vibrant health all summer.

There are crucial steps below that can be taken to create and maintain a brilliant display all through summer:

•The first step towards having a healthy container is selecting the correct size of the pot, which is determined by different factors. Choosing a small planter with crowded roots will result in less water, oxygen, and nutrients available to the roots, and all these are important for their healthy growth.

•On the other hand, when containers are too big, they will result in having excess moisture in the soil, thereby cutting off oxygen and eventually drowning the roots. Also, planters that have too much space with moist soil will help in solving most plant problems.

•In a situation where the recommended spacing is ten to twelve inches, for example, you will make sure the plants are about six to eight inches apart. Generally, if their average growth is about ten to 12 inches tall, you should opt for a pot that is nearly half the size or width of around six to eight inches. In the case of plants that grow between 24 to 36 inches tall, you will need a larger container of about 24 inches in diameter. Also, ensure your pot is composed of drainage holes with the required material below it to enable excess water are flowing out smoothly.

•It is also advisable to invert a smaller plastic pot over the drainage holes if adding more weight is an issue. There has also been some controversy as regards styrene from Styrofoam leeching into edibles. It was concluded that the low levels of styrene that are found in packaged food are due to the leaching that comes from the polystyrene containers in which they were packed. It is therefore recommended to make use of gravel, pieces of broken pottery, pebbles, nutshells, sticks, pinecones, or coffees as your drainage.

•Also, note that container plants don't like their roots sitting in water. It will result in a wet root environment that will cause most bedding plants to sulk and have low growth. They can also cause the roots to rot, which makes planters inconvenient.

•Drainage is also required to help provide your potted roots with adequate aeration. Because without this, and it will be hard for them to breathe and get easy access to oxygen.

Keeping the Bugs Out and How to Get Rid Of Bugs Naturally

Managing Pests and Plant Diseases

There are different natural and organic ways of dealing with pest and disease issues in the garden, most of which have been proved useful over recent years. In modern times, most of these techniques are usually referred to as Integrated Pest Management (IPM). They can also be related to Organic Pest Management (OPM).

For effective pest and plant disease management, close observation of your garden more often is the fundamental way to start. The ability to recognize in time that your plant is stressed will allow you to take proactive steps to help keep these pests and plant diseases in check. Nevertheless, leaving these pests and diseases unchecked will only result in an unhealthy garden with an unhealthy environment.

To help discourage these garden pests and diseases from causing damage to your garden, without having to use synthetic, non-organic controls, you are advised to consider the following techniques.

•Make sure you choose the best site and soil for the type of plants you are growing. And it will go a long way in reducing plant stress and its vulnerability to diseases and pests. If you expose your plants to excessive or too little sun, shade, fertilizer, or water, they can be stressed up. You are advised to make use of aged compost to help provide your plants with all the nutrients they need.

•You are advised to choose plant species or varieties that are resistant. Make sure you check your seed packets, including the plant labels for the pest and diseases, as well as resistance. Always try to mix different plant families to create diversity. It is useful in preventing the rapid spread of pests and plant diseases that are known for attacking specific plant groups.

•Engage in pruning or pinching to help in removing damaged or diseased leaves with branches. And it will also help in increasing the light as well as air circulation in your garden.

•You can and-pick insect pests off the plants in your container garden. You can get insects such as snails, slugs, giant adult insects, caterpillars. You can easily handpick and drop them off into soapy water.

•Make use of lures to get insects trapped using both olfactory and visual. For instance, making use of yellow sticky boards can help control whiteflies, cucumber beetles, THRIPS, and cabbage worms.

• You can make use of pest barricades such as sticky bands or floating row covers to get the pests off the plants and planting beds.

• Invite beneficial insects to your container garden. Examples of these beneficial insects include lacewings, lady beetles, and spine soldier beetles. You can also grow plants that will provide nectar and pollen for beneficial insects.

• Always keep your container garden free from plant debris. Remember that pest insects are capable of hiding or finding shelter in dropped or dead leaves. Get the soil turned during the fall or in between plantings to help expose these hidden pests.

• Bacteria, viruses, or fungi can be engaged to help kill some of these pests and garden diseases. Bacillus THURINGIENSIS is commonly used, and it is a bacteria species that gives out toxins that are poisonous to most insect pests.

• Finally, some pests and plant diseases can be controlled with the use of non-toxic sprays, such as a forceful spray of water with the garden hose to dislodge them effectively.

Ideas to Make Beautiful Containers Gardening

Fun ways to make and decorate containers with kids

Finding boxes can be a lot of fun. They can be painted and decorated and it could be a great activity for kids too, who will enjoy making excellent pots out of everyday things.

Look in your garage for things you can use. Look around your house. Try to find unusual objects to use in the garden. Almost anything can be a planter! The more unique it is, the funnier it will be.

There are many ways you can decorate containers; you can paint them, you can attach cool things to them, you can draw on them and you can build them out of different materials. Let's look at some different ways you can decorate your containers.

Painting

You can use tempera paints on many different materials to make them beautiful. You can free paint on your containers. You can paint each box a different color, or you can paint them all the same color. You can paint abstract shapes on the containers. You can paint rainbows or polka dots. You can paint a scene in the garden. You can paint pictures of the people who work in the garden. You can paint pictures of the vegetables growing in each container, which is also an excellent way to remember what you are growing in each box! You can paint your containers however you like - there is no wrong way to do it!

Stencils

You can use stencils to make patterns on the containers. To make a simple stencil, draw a star or other dull object on a manila file folder. Then place the stencil against the box and fill it in with paint. You can also use spray paint to do this quickly. One stencil can be used to decorate an entire container with lots of stars! What other shapes can you think of that would be excellent stencils?

Drawing

Just like painting, you can use permanent markers to draw on your containers. If your box is too dark for drawing, you can spray paint it white first. You can also paint it another light color. Then, you can draw on it, or write your name on it, or write an explanation of what is in the pot. You can even write what kind of plant it is, and how to take care for it!

Found objects

You can look around your house and garden to find objects to attach to the containers. If you do this, be sure to paint over them with clear lacquer. Lacquer will seal the images in and protect them from the rain. Have a grownup help you with this part. Try to think of other neat things you can glue to your containers.

Of course, each container can be a combination of these techniques. For instance, you might want to paint or draw a scene of a garden on your vessel. You can make a stencil in the shape of corn plants to add them to the stage. Then you could glue a picture of yourself in the garden, and glue dried beans to show the bean plant! Be creative and think of ways you can mix and match the different ways to decorate your container.

Building containers

You can also build neat boxes from various materials. When you do so, be sure to think creatively about how they will look as well as how they will work. Artists call thinking this way, combining *form* and *function*. The structure is how the container looks and service is how it works. If you approach your content creation with form and function in mind, you will have a serene looking container garden that works well!

Making Containers from Recycled Materials

Cut the bottom off a milk jug. Turn the jug upside down. Then, thread a seedling that is at least four or five inches tall through the top of the jar. Be sure to keep the seedling in its root ball when you do this. Fill the rest of the jug at least halfway with soil. Punch holes in the sides of the jar at least four inches from the bottom. You can reinforce the holes with grommets. Make at least three holes, so the jug is balanced. Then, attach ropes or twine to the pits and hang the jar. Water normally. You can also make larger upside-down pots from buckets. As always, be creative!

Another kind of container is called a grow bag. It is what it sounds like: a bag for growing vegetables! You can buy grow bags at garden supply stores or make your own. The easiest way to make a grow bag is with a reusable shopping bag. These bags will hold their form and should not fall over. The shopping bag is porous so that air will reach the roots, and water will drain quickly. Because water flows so smoothly, be sure to check the container at least once a day to make sure it does not dry out. An extra advantage of using a shopping bag is that it has handled - so you can move it around quickly! Be sure to use a sturdy material like canvas. Cheap reusable bags may tear from the weight of the soil. Grow bags are best for growing small or medium-sized vegetables like tomatoes and peppers.

Creative containers

Let's get creative with our containers. Anything can be a container. Look around - you can find boxes everywhere that you can use in your garden!

Once you have decided what you are going to plant, you need to find out what size containers you need. Make a list of the vegetables you will grow. Then make a list of boxes. Your listing should say whether the containers you need are small, medium, or large. Once you know how many of each kind you need, start looking!

Very small plants do not need much room to grow and thrive. For these plants, like lettuce, radishes or carrots, small containers will do. You can use coffee cans with holes punched in the bottom. Or you can cut the tops off of milk jugs. Keep reading for more ideas about what you can use to make containers.

Anything can be a container if it is sturdy, holds water, and can be drained. What that means is that the walls should be strong enough to hold a lot of wet soil, which is cumbersome. It should also not leak through the sides. And it can be drained if you can make holes in the bottom of it. That means that glass or solid concrete containers do not work well. If the box does not drain, the plant will not grow properly.

If you are using containers with a porous material, they might need to be lined. "Porous" materials have tiny holes in them and can absorb water. Wood is an example of a porous material. If the wood is soaked in water, it will absorb it. It will make the wood soft and rotten over time, which will ruin your container. You can find out if a material is porous by pouring water on it. If you can wipe all of the water off with a cloth, it is not porous. If you wipe it off and the material stays wet, it is probably porous.

Some materials, like terra cotta, are porous but are not damaged by becoming wet. Still, they can have leftover minerals or even plant diseases in them. If you buy used terra cotta pots, be sure to clean them before you use them. You can kill any infections in them by baking them at 225 F for an hour. Be sure to open the windows while you do this, as it can get smelly!

You can line wooden containers with plastic sheets or garbage bags. Poke holes in the bottom of the plastic so that water can drain. Terra cotta pots do not have to be lined. If you choose to do so, you can use plastic pot liners that are made just for this purpose.

You can also buy upside-down containers for growing vegetables like tomatoes or peppers. These are fun to grow in. They are also more relaxed. Upside-down plants do not need stakes or cages to hold them up. Pests have a hard time finding upside-down planters. You can buy upside-down planters that come with everything you need at the garden store. Or you can make your own out of milk jugs.

Toxic materials

Please make sure not to use containers with toxic materials for your boxes. Water and soil can leach poisonous substances right into your plants. Some stuff we do not apply for containers is treated wood, old barrels that carried toxic chemicals, certain art supplies, and any box that might contain a poisonous residue. If in doubt, don't use it!

Tips and Tricks for Container Gardening

Container gardening is less expensive than maintaining a regular garden; however, it can still cost you a lot. By merely planning how you would go about with your container gardening, you could cut the cost by half. How do you do this?

Tips on How to Reduce Container Gardening Costs

Tips When Setting a Budget

Assess why you are into container gardening. It is the foundation of your garden. If your motive is to earn, then you can plan the plants that you are going to have, the materials that you would need and other pertinent data. However, if you have no solid reasons why you are into this, you would just do things without regard to the future, and you might spend unnecessarily. If you have finally decided why you are bent on having container gardening, then you can do smart planning.

Write down your plans. You would see the overall picture when you write down your thoughts, strategies, ideas and blueprint of your garden. You would also be able to list down all the things you would need when you have a picture of your plans and not just a mental image. Plus, you could estimate the timeframe you need to complete your garden.

Make a to-buy list ahead of time and keep an eye on the costs. You can check how much you would need when you plan your garden needs. You could do your shopping at the end of the season sales and save money. Buy the items and supplies that you need throughout the year and store them until they are required. When you do not know the things you need for the whole year, you tend to buy them according to the time you need them, and that could be costly for you.

Study how you would go about your plans. You can ask the opinions of other garden experts or enthusiasts or ask for help from friends or other people you know who are into container gardening. You could adjust your plans when you acquire better suggestions or ideas.

Thorough planning would save you money and cause you to spend less than necessary for your container gardening.

10 Tips to lessen your container gardening expenses

Start from seeds.

Most seeds cost less than a dollar. If you would start from scratch, it may take some time and more effort, but you would save a lot. As you go looking for seeds for your container garden, you might find be confused with some of the terms used for describing seeds. For your clarification:

- F1 varieties or hybrids. It is the expensive seeds as the process of producing these seeds is more complicated than usual. The crossing of two-parent varieties is done so that a new one will be created.
- Genetically modified. These seeds are created in the laboratories where their genes are manipulated.
- Open-pollinated varieties. Also known as heirloom varieties, these seeds can be reused year after year. They are found to be more resistant to various crop diseases.
- Organic seed. Grown without the use of pesticides, fungicides, herbicides, or fertilizers.

For newbies, choose the "easy seeds" to plant. These are hardy and easy to plant, plus they grow earlier, too.

Buy seedlings.

Having healthy, young plants also cost less in the long run. They have a higher probability of surviving than seeds. Lesser efforts are required to ensure that they survive the transfer to another occasion. When buying seedlings, make sure to check the leaves; they should be green, and if there are patches of white or dried leaves, avoid these plants as they could mean weak or unhealthy plants. They may not last long when you transplant them. Check also if they are firmly attached to a group. Trying to separate and plant them could cause trauma to the plant and cause its death. Those planted singly are easier to transplant and have a higher probability of surviving a transplant. Also, do not just depend on the height of the plants to determine if they can survive. It has been noticed that smaller plants do better at staying alive when transplanted.

Buy all your garden needs during the sale.

It usually takes place every end of the growing season. At this time, containers are marked down at half prices. Even other supplies such as tools and decorative supplies would cost less. Therefore, if you have any garden need that can wait until the clearance sales, acquire them during that time and save money.

Propagate your seedlings.

Some seedlings are effortless to propagate. Instead of buying many of these plants, just be the one to multiply them and save money. Look for plants that can be spread only by simply cutting branches and putting them in water. When roots start to come from those branches, plant them in containers or pots. There is even something better than this. Some plants just propagate on-their-own. All you have to do is to transplant them when they are strong enough to be transferred to a different container from the mother plant.

Recycle.

Instead of buying containers, take a closer look at things in your house. Maybe there are old pails that you can use as pots. Old baskets can be redecorated and be used as vases in your container gardening. Be creative and imaginative and transform those old buckets or bottles into something useful. You would discover that there are many things in your house (specifically in your attic or basement) that can be recycled and converted into garden items.

Exchange seeds or seedlings with others.

Instead of looking and buying seeds and seedlings from garden centers, contact friends who are garden container enthusiasts and strike a deal with them. You can trade seeds and seedlings. You would not have to spend money at all, plus that is also building camaraderie with other gardeners.

Make your compost.

Instead of buying fertilizers, you can make your compost in your backyard. Simply dig a small portion, and leftovers and other biodegradable things can be placed there. Not only have you saved money for fertilizer or compost, but you have also helped the environment by cutting the garbage being sent to landfills.

Compare and contrast prices.

You can save money when you try to check different stores, flea markets, yard sales, and thrift stores. Sometimes, one tends to patronize a specific store, and he or she misses other great deals at different stores. You can also check online for the most significant sales and best offers of different shops. Look for coupons or vouchers too in your daily newspapers.

Choose edible plants.

Instead of buying exotic and expensive plants, be practical and buy things that you could use in your kitchen. You do not only save money on caring for those strange plants, but you also save grocery money when you harvest your vegetables or herbs in your container garden. Think of all the herbs and vegetables that you always need in your kitchen like garlic, ginger, parsley or celery and plant them. Whenever you need any of these, you do not have to shell out cash. Just go to your garden and harvest from them. Plus, this might motivate you to start a little business and increase your income all the more.

Neighbors or friends could just order some of your products instead of buying them in the local grocery stores. You could also try edible flowers. That way, you have house décor and ingredients for dishes at the same time.

Place an ad, use your social media accounts or the word of mouth advertisement and just inform other people that you are into container gardening.

You would be amazed at how sometimes people just offer many tips, items or even plants for you, for free. For some people, instead of having tools or gardening supplies that are not being used in their homes or just adding spaces in their garage or sheds, they would instead give them to other garden enthusiasts if they know they require those. You save money, and at the same time, you have helped those people dispose of the items they consider as junk in their homes.

One does not need to spend so much. Be wise and use these tips and see how much you can save by doing so.

Preparing Your Tools and Supplies

After you have decided and researched what you will grow in your container garden, the following step would be to collect the gardening tools the supplies that you will need. Once you have done that, you will then move on to preparing all of your containers.

Gardening Tools and Supplies

You will need some essential tools and planting materials to make the maintenance and care of your container garden a pleasant and productive experience.

At a garden center, purchase planting bagged planting materials, including topsoil, organic mulch and compost. These are usually sold in volume or cubic feet. Use an online calculator for gardeners to find out how much you will need. Most calculators will require you to type in the dimensions of your gardening area and how dense you want your planting material to be.

Since you will be working with a container garden, you are going to need hand tools for gardening. Aim for quality, since most devices are well worth the price. The necessary tools that you will need to start with are a pair of gardening gloves. A watering can, a small trowel or a three-pronged fork, and a compost scoop.

If you want to build up your gardening tool collection, consider the following: secateurs (a specific pair of scissors for trimming and pruning), a dibber (to create more precise holes for your seeds), and a soil sieve. You should also have a dustpan and brush to sweep up soil that gets spilled over your containers.

Garden Center Shopping Tips

You can get your seeds or seedlings at a local farmers' market or nursery. There will be a wide array of vegetable choices, so make sure to bring a list of the ones you have selected to avoid feeling overwhelmed.

In choosing seedlings, check the textures, leaf colors and the roots. Avoid plants that have brown or notched leaf edges, papery, bleached leaves, and too many scars and broken stems. Also, check the care tags to verify if the seedlings can grow with other plants in the same container.

It is advised that you visit the nursery on a weekday so that the salesperson will be able to accommodate you better and answer all of your questions. Frequently, the plants are organized based on the conditions that enable them to grow well, such as "sunny or dry" and "shade tolerant." Choose the appropriate ones based on your available area.

Prepare your Containers

Before planting your seedlings and seeds, you will need to prepare your potting mix. The first step is to make sure that all of the containers are clean and free from any contaminants that might harm your plants, such as insect repellent spray. Check the drainage holes to see if there is enough to prevent the soil from getting soaked. You do not have to place gravel or pot shards in the bottom of the containers; instead, set a layer of newspaper to prevent the potting mix from spilling. If your receptacle is too deep, one way to minimize the amount of potting mix that you will use is to place some gravel in the bottom.

Make sure to prepare your potting mix outdoors as potting soil can irritate your lungs, skin and eyes.

Do not use plain garden soil for your container garden, as this is too dense. Instead, mix houseplant soil mixture with your loamy soil. There are plenty of commercial planting mixes available at garden centers. You can also come up with your mix at home by combining compost with pulverized perlite, vermiculite, pine or fir bark. For every cubic foot of mix, include (4 Oz) of dolomitic limestone, (4 Oz) of greensand, (2 Oz) of blood meal, (1 lb.) of rock phosphate or colloidal phosphate, and (1 lb.) of granite dust. As you fill up each container, leave at least 1 inch of space between the surface of the soil and the rim of the box so that you can leave room for watering.

After you have mixed the potting soil, the following step is to pre-moisten it by watering it several times and then mixing it some more. The soil should be consistently moist before you start planting.

Tips for Starting Seeds

Depending on the type and quality of the seeds you're trying to get started, starting your seeds can be a rewarding experience, or it can be frustrating to the point of tears. It's exhilarating to check on your seeds to find they've sprouted overnight, and there's nothing better than watching a seed you've sprouted grow into a mature plant complete with tasty vegetables. On the other hand, sometimes you can do everything in your power to bring your seeds to life, only to have them not sprout or sprout, but fail to grow into healthy plants.

Seeds should be started according to the manufacturer's instructions. These instructions are usually found on the seed packet and are often the best way to give your seeds a great shot at life. After all, it benefits a manufacturer when you're able to get their grains to grow because you're likely to purchase from them again in the future.

To get up and to run, your seeds need three things:

- Healthy soil.

- Water.

- Light.

Although one could reasonably surmise seeds should be able to sprout in any soil since they're designed to propagate naturally, having the right soil blend will give your seedlings a better shot at life. While the perfect soil blend is dependent on the type of seed being planted, the following mix works well for most seed types:

- 4 parts perlite.

- 4 parts sphagnum moss.

- 1 part worm castings.

If worm castings aren't available, you can use equal parts perlite and sphagnum moss to good effect. Seedlings do best in soil that hasn't had fertilizer added. You can add it if you want, but wait until they get their second set of leaves. Most seedlings grow best when the soil temperature is kept between 65 and 70 degrees F.

In addition to good soil, your seeds are going to need light, and lots of it.

If you're starting your seeds indoors, the ambient light in the house probably isn't going to be enough. You can set up a small artificial lighting system to make sure your plants get the view they need. Use a combination of fresh and warm fluorescent bulbs and set them on a timer, so your plants get at least 14 hours of light a day. The lights need to be set up, so they're only a few inches away from the plants.

Follow the planting instruction on the seed packet when setting your seeds in the soil. Some seeds are supposed to be broadcast onto the surface of the land. Some need to be placed just below the surface, while others do best when placed an inch or more into the ground. Some seeds need to be oriented in a specific direction to ensure proper growth.

After planting your seeds, you need to keep the soil around them damp, but not soaking wet. Moist, well-drained soil is conducive to seed-starting. Let your soil dry out, and you're going to reduce the number of seeds that sprout drastically. It is problematic because the small pots that seeds are typically started in are tough to keep moist, especially if they're being kept under warm lights. If you're like me and tend to forget to water your plants, a self-watering system can be a lifesaver. These systems take the guesswork out of watering because they water your plants for you and will keep your seeds beautiful and damp the way they need to be to sprout.

If you're using tap water to water your plants, let the water warm up to room temperature before using it. Don't use water that's passed through a water softener because it will contain too much sodium. Chlorinated water needs to be left out overnight to get rid of the chlorine.

Plants that are started outside tend to be healthier because they're exposed to the elements from an early age. They're forced to develop stronger roots and a thicker stem to withstand the wind. You can simulate this effect indoors by setting up a fan in your grow area and letting it blow a gentle breeze across your seedlings for a few hours a day.

Some plants don't lend themselves well to being transplanted, and their seeds have to be started in the containers in which they're going to be grown.

When you're using smaller containers, this isn't a problem because you can bring the boxes inside to get the seeds started. When planting in larger vessels that aren't mobile, you may have to start your seeds outdoors. Make sure you follow the manufacturer's recommendations and avoid planting your seeds too early. If your seeds are exposed to excessively cold weather while germinating, they may not sprout. If they do germinate, the seedlings will be stressed out and probably won't grow into healthy plants.

Damping Off

Amongst the issues that can crop up and affect seedling growth, damping off is the most prevalent. It is a disease brought about by the growth of fungus that can cause stop germination dead in its tracks and can kill off seedlings in a hurry. Damping-off can kill seeds before they emerge from the ground, or it can kill young seedlings after they sprout.

The following symptoms are indicative of damping-off:

- Dying seedlings.

- Leaf spotting.

- Mold on the surface of your soil.

- Rotting roots.

- Seedlings that turns black.

- Seeds that won't sprout.

- Thin seedlings.

- Thin stems.

- Wiry seedlings.

Several fungi types can cause damping off. These fungi live in the ground and can start growing and attacking your plants if conditions are right. Damping-off usually takes place in localized patches and spreads outward in a circle. If you notice some of your seedlings are dying off, getting rid of the tray that's damping off can stop the disease from spreading.

The best way to prevent damping off is to use clean soil from trusted sources. Sterilize your containers before use and keep your seed trays in a clean, sterile area. Don't use the same gloves and tools on your seedlings that you use in your garden because you risk introducing new fungi to your soil.

Unless you're using sterilized soil, there will always be some fungi in your soil. It isn't necessarily a bad thing, as long as you're able to keep the bad mushrooms in check. You can do this by using soil that drains well and doesn't hold too much water. There's a fine line between keeping your soil damp and saturating it with water. Cross the front, and you're creating conditions conducive to the growth of the harmful fungus that causes damping off.

Vigorous seedlings and plants will be less susceptible to fungi, so be sure to give your plants what they need to overgrow. Make sure soil temperatures are correct, give them the exact amount of light and make sure they get the water they need, but no more than what's necessary. Damping-off is no longer a concern once plants make it through the seedling stage and mature into adult plants.

Harvesting and Storing Your Crop

The most enjoyable part of container gardening starts when the fruit has ripened, and it is time to harvest the crop. It is the time when you sample your produce as you are watering and enjoy the benefits of all your hard work.

Root vegetables are easy to harvest; just pull them up, cut off the leaves and prepare the plant! If you have used the soil mix, then it is easy to pull up your root vegetables with no digging. These will typically be okay in the ground for several weeks once ripe, meaning you can pull them up as and when you need them rather than removing all at once.

With your other plants, the fruits are likely to be ready at different times. Typically with tomatoes, for example, the fruits are not all ripe on the same day. They ripen over time, so you have to check the plants and remove the ripe fruit before they go past their best. Be careful how you delete them as pulling at the plant could damage it and introduce disease.

Any vegetable that grows on a stalk can either be removed by cutting with scissors or a knife (very carefully) or pinching it between your finger and nails. You need a clean cut so that you do not introduce infection into your plant.

Once your vegetables are overripe, the taste can start to deteriorate; tomatoes become squishy, root vegetables grow woody and so on. You need to keep an eye on your veggies, so they do not go past their best.

Harvest Your Crop When You Will Use It

You should only harvest your vegetables when you are going to use them or if you are going to use them in the following day or two as most home-grown produce, particularly soft vegetables, do not store well. It is because they are not covered in the chemicals that are used by the commercial growers to preserve them. Your crop will stay fresher longer on the plants or in the ground than they will, in general, in your refrigerator.

However, should you have vegetables that are going past their prime, then you will need to harvest them and either stores them or make something from them; otherwise, they can rot on the plants or attract unwanted pests.

There are lots of dishes you can make with your excess produce, and you can certainly enjoy a few weeks of delicious cooking from the fruits of your labor.

Freeze Your Excess Produce

Most other vegetables can be frozen, with potatoes being one of the main exceptions. Potatoes can be stored for several months in paper bags in a cool dark place. Onions can be cooked and frozen though they too will store in a cool dark place for many months if dried and hung. Grow enough of these, and they can easily supply you through the winter months.

Vegetables can be frozen by blanching them to remove bacteria and then plunging them into icy cold water to stop the cooking process. These can be put into portion-sized containers and frozen as a "lump," or you can spread them on trays, freeze them and then bag them up afterward. Most vegetables only need blanching for 30 to 60 seconds with harder plants needing longer blanching times than softer ones.

Be Creative with Your Excess Produce

Of course, there is much more you can do with your crop other than just freeze it. Some people will prepare meals with their products and freeze the meals, or you can make jams, chutneys, sauces or pickles, depending on what you have an excess.

If I have too many tomatoes, then I tend to make either tomato ketchup, tomato soup or tomato sauce for pasta. When I have an excess of root vegetables, I will usually make a massive batch of stew and then freeze the finished product in portion-sized containers for quick ready meals. Fruits like strawberries get turned in to jams, and my herbs are dried and stored in boxes for use throughout the year.

If you are adventurous, then many fruits and vegetables that you grow at home can be made into wine, which is an interesting alternative use for a bumper harvest

If you do not have the time to do anything with your excess crop, you are bound to have friends, family and neighbors who would be more than happy to receive your excess fresh produce. If you prefer, you could even donate them to a soup kitchen or food bank.

Just remember to be careful to avoid damaging your plants when harvesting the crop. If the frosts are coming, you will need to collect whatever is left of your vegetables, so they do not get damaged. You can store your plants or use them to make dishes that are then frozen or preserved for enjoyment during the winter months.

Drying and Preserving Herbs

Harvesting herbs is one of the best moments in gardening. It is when you get to appreciate all your efforts and patience for gardening. However, you can't use all of these herbs at the same time, and you can't delay harvesting it either. Some herbs need to be entirely uprooted to be collected while you have to pick out all the flowers and leaves of some. Otherwise, they will no longer be as fresh and tasty when used for cooking.

That's why you must learn how to preserve herbs. Preserved herbs last longer and can be stored and used all year round. Preserving herbs usually includes drying, freezing, dehydrating or mixing them in oil.

These preservation methods are relatively easy and do not require the use of complicated tools and materials. All the materials you'll need can be found in your kitchen. Here's how you can preserve your herbs.

1. Harvesting – before you preserve your herbs, you need to harvest the edible parts of the plant. Take scissors or a knife and use it to cut the stems, leaves or flowers of the herb. After collecting the herbs, wash it with water. Gently spray it with water and let it dry by patting it with a paper towel or napkin. It's best to immediately proceed with preserving the herbs to maintain the shape and color of the herbs.

2. Maintain the Appearance – some herbs change appearance when preserved. It changes its color, its shape and size. However, some herbs can retain their appearance:

a. Herbs with sharp leaves are more natural to preserve since the sheets do not deform easily. They can maintain their color and shape. Some good examples are rosemary, thyme and sage.

b. Herbs with tender and soft leaves are a bit trickier since the leaves can change shape, size and color. Herbs like parsley, basil and mint fall under this category.

Some herbs are better used fresh than dried, but trial and error is the best way to determine which herbs you'll preserve.

After all, you might find a specific herb better used when preserved than when it is fresh. Personal preferences will also affect your decision when it comes to choosing which herbs you'll maintain.

3. Drying – this is the most common and popular method of preserving herbs. There are several ways to dry herbs. Some of the methods are hanging, towel drying, air drying, outdoor drying, drying using a microwave or oven, natural drying, drying through the use of desiccants and drying by pressing.

4. Hanging – this involved hanging the herbs in a dark area. Its method is also used in preserving flowers like roses. It will take a couple of days before the herbs are completely dried up. To do this, take the herbs you wish to dry and tie them in groups. Attach a string around the stems. Its line must be long enough to hang the herbs upside down. Take the herbs and hang them in a relaxed and dark area like a closet or kitchen cabinet. Make sure that the wardrobe and offices are clean and free of pests and insects to avoid damages. Check after a couple of days. The leaves should be dry with a brittle texture.

5. Towel Drying – take the herbs and a clean towel. Place the sheet on a clean and flat surface. After washing and cleaning the herbs, lay the herbs on the cloth. Do not overcrowd the herbs on one towel. It works best when there's enough space between each herb. Set aside and leave the herbs on the sheet until completely dry.

6. Air Drying – similar to hanging, but except for a closet. Take the herbs and tie them in bundles and groups. Make sure that each package is of the same herb variety and size. Make sure to hang the herbs upside down, with the flowers and leaves facing downwards. It will help in drying all the moisture in the grass. Put the herbs in separate paper bags and secure the end with a string. The paper bag speeds up the drying process and, at the same time, catches falling leaves, flowers or seeds which you can use in the future. Hang the herbs and remove them when they are dehydrated.

7. Outdoor Drying –take the herbs and tie them in bundles. Put them inside a paper bag and secure the ends. The paper bag will prevent the herbs from being too dried up, which can cause the herbs to lose their flavor. Then, hang the herbs outside where there is direct sunlight. Its method is perfect for drying herbs intended for craft and DIY projects.

8. Drying Using an Oven or Microwave – if you don't have the patience of waiting for days for the herbs to dry, you can use an oven or microwave to speed up the drying process. Take the herbs and place them on a rack lined with baking paper. Make sure that the herbs do not touch each other. Put them inside the oven or microwave and set it on the lowest setting possible. Dry in the oven or microwave for about a minute. After that, take the herbs and check if they're dried completely. If not, add another 30 seconds. Once the herbs are dried, store them for future use.

9. Natural Drying – natural drying allows the herbs to dry in a container. Though this is not the best way to dry herbs, it works well with rosemary and fennel. Take the herbs and place them in a box. Arrange the herbs properly and leave the container in a warm and dry place. Check regularly and monitor for any signs of damages like mildew.

10. Use of Desiccant – desiccant are substances that drain moisture from an object. A good example would be silica gel, sand and borax. Take the herbs, the desiccant and a bowl. Cover the base of the container with desiccant and place the herbs on it. After that, add another layer of desiccant on the grass. Set aside and check once in a while to see if the herbs are already dry.

11. Pressing – simply take the herbs and place them between pages of note. Close the text and add some weight on top of it. After a few days, the herbs are pressed and dried. It is perfect for crafts and artworks.

12. Freezing – another method of preserving herbs is by freezing. Its process works best with herbs with soft and tender leaves like basil, mint and lemon balm. Take the herbs and wash them thoroughly. Boil some water and dip the herbs to blanch them. Afterward, put the herbs straight into ice-cold water and freeze. Blanching your herbs will help them last up to six months.

13. Preserve in Oil – use natural and organic oil in preserving the herbs. The most suitable oil is olive oil. Take the herbs and wash them thoroughly. Pat dry with a paper towel and put it inside a jar. Pour oil into the pot, making sure that all the herbs are covered and submerged in oil. Secure the jar and refrigerate.

These methods are effortless and easy to follow. Aside from that, preserving helps in retaining the original color and flavor of the herbs. Just make sure to wash the herbs thoroughly before preserving them. Remove damaged leaves or flowers. Cut the herbs in the same length and sizes and always group them with their variety. It's also recommended that you have separate jars for each type of preserved herbs.

Herb Gardening

When planting herbs at home, there are important tips that will help you achieve success even without experience in gardening. Some of these tips include;

Tip #1: Determine the herbs that you would like to plant starting with the simplest trio of basil, rosemary and oregano or chives.

Tip #2: Ensure that you do your gardening in a suitable location, whether out in the garden or a container, so that the herbs have access to maximum conditions that support their growth.

Tip #3: Buy seeds from reputable companies to ensure that you are handling herbs whose genetic makeup is intact.

Tip #4: To preserve the nutritional content of your herbs, you can do drying and freeze, among other methods of preservation.

Frequently Asked Questions about Herb Gardening

Which herbs can I begin with?

The truth is, hundreds of herbs are available in repositories, and you can cultivate for their medicinal and culinary benefits. However, the most important factors that you have to consider when choosing the right herbs will be what you want to grow, and other essential conditions that support your herbs of choice such as the soil and the climate.

The best thing is for you to assess a list of herbs that you have in mind and determine which ones you are your favorite and fit into the growth conditions available in your location.

What cultural requirements do the herbs have?

For each herb to thrive well, you must know the required conditions for their optimal growth. Other plants also can self-propagate, in which case you are fortunate if one of your herbs does this. Self-propagation refers to the ability of a plant to self-reproduce either by reseeding, layering, cutting, among other ways.

The most important thing is to pay close attention to the amount of sun the herbs need each day. The information that you can get from journals, and if it says that they need it for 4-6 hours in a day, then it probably needs just that! The other thing is water requirements and the soil type it needs. It ensures that they get optimal conditions for optimal growth and development.

Which herbs can I start within my weather?

When it comes to the choice of herbs to plant in your climate, you can replicate each herb's requirements. For instance, most of the herbs do well with less water, 4-6 hours of sunlight exposure and average quality soil.

However, when it comes to winter temperatures, the conditions cannot be compromised. It means that you have to be within the zone that your herbs of choice can thrive. You can also find this information available at the nursery where these herb seedlings are raised.

The truth is, determining the kinds of herbs that will do well within your area. You will realize that is you come from a place where the conditions are delicate; you can grow a few of those that need this kind of terms specifically. You can also substitute those you cannot grow in your area.

Should I raise my herbs from seeds?

Seeds are the best when it comes to herb gardening, especially if you are a beginner. Remember that we have mentioned getting seeds from reputable companies that have not genetically engineered their components. In fact, rather than getting your seeds just from one company, you can get them from at least two companies.

It is also crucial that you ensure that you have read the herb's descriptions well.

The best thing is to consider a suitable vendor to work. To do that, consider asking yourself the following questions;

Which company meets the criteria you are looking?

Will the company be a suitable resource for educational materials?

If their process of ordering helpful?

What is their client service?

Do they have ethical considerations when it comes to GMOs, hybrid seeds and SEMINIS?

Don't worry if you feel like you are not ready yet to raise herbs from seeds. The truth is that you will finally get where you are going, and the best thing is for you to start with the goal in mind.

Where can I find herb plants?

If you desire to start a medicinal or culinary herb garden, there is a good chance that you will exhaust so many resources available in local nurseries within a couple of years. It is because, by the time you have mastered all that information, you will already be herb-savvy! It is because you will have moved from pure herbs like basil to a broader and more intricate variety.

However, if you are specifically looking for culinary and medicinal herbs, the best place you can get them is from Horizon Herbs. The best thing with this place is that they offer you satisfactory answers to your questions that revolve around; what seeds are viable. They also have packets, catalogs, and experts who are knowledgeable about herbs. They sell container herbs and cuttings from the roots, which can be very helpful, especially if you do not wish to start from growing seeds.

Can I grow herbs from seeds?

If you have a friend, family or local nursery growing herbs, you can gather information from them on the best methods of rooting or cutting for that particular herb and then try to replicate the same.

For instance, what I have found out about thyme over the years is that they can be propagated so well and easily by layering. It is how you can achieve successful layering by first taking a supple thyme stem that is mature and sits it in the soil.

Use a garden pin to weight that down. Ensure that you have it watered well and then wait for it to begin sprouting at the soil surface. Then cut it off to get new herbs. Hence no seed required.

Again, you must ensure that you have reference material on hand. It is also vital for you to learn how to perform wild crafts, especially for those plants that you have available and where it is legal.

Amount of space needed

Here, the best answer is for you to determine what space you have available for herb gardening. If you live in an urban apartment, you must consider what to grow in your deck, window or patio facing the southern direction.

On the other hand, you may have a friend that has a farm backyard or an extra space in their yard that they can give you to grow your herbs. After all, it is said, if you are into herb gardening, you have to get in touch with your creative self. The bottom line is for you to look for sufficient space to cultivate your herbs.

When determining the amount of space you need for your herbs; you have to ask yourself:

Are there people growing this herb?

How many plants will take the available space?

How much space is enough for the herbs you intend to plant? If their lots of shade, unusable ground or is the entire space available?

What you have to note is that you need to know your herbs well and work with your plan. The truth is that it does not matter how much time it takes for the grasses to mature. What truly matters is being able to use that time well to learn more about herbal preparations, their uses, and properties. You have to be willing to know your herbs themselves as they grow and when they occasionally fail.

My advice is that you should take your time and pace yourself. But what is even relevant is for you to start this year and start planning and planting your herbal garden. It does not matter how small the effort is; the key is for you to grow what you will use and what will grow. The sooner you embrace container gardening, the better for you will be at this.

General Upkeep

Apart from watering and fertilizing, what else does the vegetable container garden need? Consider the following tasks:

•Staking and framework - You may have chosen plants that require some support or other form of climbing apparatus. Be sure that you install these things at the time you plant seeds or transplants. Be sure that you are using safe plant materials to tie these plants to their growing structures, and to continually gauge them for their ratio of above the soil growth/weight to below the soil counterweights.

•Deadheading - A lot of container gardeners forget that some of their plants will need pruning and deadheading if they are to produce the number of blooms or produce indicated. Take the time to discover what the best methods might be. For instance, you will want to know how to pinch or prune tomatoes to keep them at the level of control you require. The same can be said for many plants and flowers, so do a bit of research to discover what is best for your plants.

•Monitor for pests - There is little that you can do to prevent pests from finding your plants, so be as vigilant about them with your container gardens as possible. Because the world of a single container is so small, a single invasion of caterpillars or insects can decimate the miniature garden in a matter of days or even hours. Be aware of signs of disease, too, as this can mean that a contagious problem is at hand. Quarantine any containers that seem to be affected and take all possible action as soon as you notice any issues.

•Consider reflections - Many container gardeners forget that heat and light can be a bit overwhelming to potted plants. For example, a container garden on a patio paved with white stones or concrete is getting sunlight from almost every angle. It is because the light is reflecting upon the plants as well as shining from above. Try to keep this sort of double threat in mind and provide plants with shade, if possible.

•Have emergency plans - Do you live in an area prone to violent thunderstorms, hail, or other extremes? If so, try to consider what this might mean to the container garden. If you can offer some sort of protection when severe weather, or even early frosts, are forecast, it can save a lot of heartbreak and waste.

•Replacements - If you took our advice about making succession plantings to keep yourself supplied with things all season, be sure that you are preparing the soil for each new crop. Try not to double up on the same item on the same ground over and over again during the summer. Make some plans to have replacements ready, but to make them different than the plants before them. It helps to keep the soil in your containers as healthy and rich as possible and also cut back on the risks of disease.

You will get into a good rhythm with the container garden. You will find that it becomes a charming habit to head to the various pots and containers to see what might be ready to eat, how individual plants are doing, and just to enjoy the sights, smells, and textures of growing things.

Unfortunately, like most good things, your garden will have to reach its end as the season's change. The growing season may last 3/4 of the year where you are, or it could be less than 1/3 of the year. No matter what, you will have a lot of end of season tasks to consider.

These will include:

•Removing frost killed or depleted plants from the containers - start a wonderful compost heap by tossing all of the dead or expired plants into the mix, and also consider using the potting soil in a pile as well.

•Empty pots and scrub them clean with a bleach mixture (10% works best) to ensure that no fungal issues remain.

•Put fragile or vulnerable pots into storage.

• Prepare overwintering plants by surrounding heavy or immovable planters that contain perennials and woody plants with straw and wrapping with burlap. (Note: You can avoid the need to do this by using smaller containers inside oversized containers and simply lifting the potted plants out for overwintering in more controlled conditions such as a root cellar or insulated garden shed)

• Dig a protective trench for smaller plants in containers and place them in the channel, covered with soil and straw for the winter months. Water them in well until the first frosts arrive. (Note: This will not work with clay pots. Simply remove their plants and lay the plants in the trench with the other potted plants, and store the clay vessels indoors)

Once the garden has been prepared for colder weather, you can start to make plans for the upcoming season. Many container gardeners spend happy hours during the winter months looking through seed and plant catalogs and developing strategies to expand their garden during the following season.

Conclusion

Thank you for making it to the end. While fertilizing, watering and weeding are the big three, there are still a few maintenance tasks which you are going to need to do if you want to keep your garden healthy. There are also a couple tasks that you'll have to do if you want to make sure that your harvest goes smoothly and the veggies themselves are high quality. None of these tasks will take you very long, and a few of them only need to be done once, maybe twice, per crop. But skipping out on these tasks is a bad idea as doing so needlessly puts your garden at risk.

Some of these tasks could arguably be considered pest control and disease prevention techniques, such as removing dead plant matter which could harbor both. They are important enough to merit a discussion here as well. You should be building your pest control behaviors into your general garden maintenance routine so that you are never caught unprepared by an unexpected infestation or infection.

Always remember to disinfect your tools after use. This is a common sense maintenance task that you wouldn't believe how many gardeners ignore. The reason it is ignored is likely one of ignorance and a lack of knowledge. Plants are living creatures. They not only have a living biology but they can communicate their needs to us in their visual language. You should disinfect all of your tools, including your shovels, rakes or hoes. Still, you especially need to disinfect shears or anything else that has come into contact with the plants themselves. Trimming a plant is essentially a form of surgery. Imagine going in for an operation and finding out the surgeon used a dirty scalpel to cut you open. You wouldn't be surprised at all when the wound got infected or you caught a new disease. Yet many gardeners leave their tools dirty and use them again and again, only to be surprised when their plants end up sick. Always disinfect your tools at the end of the day after using them.

Remove Dead Plant Matter. Another step that is often forgotten about is the removal of dead plant matter. A lot of beginner gardeners don't see a problem with a dead plant matter in their beds, but leaving dead plant matter in and around your garden is one of the worst things you can do if you want your plants to stay healthy. The problem isn't the dead matter itself. The plant matter is dead; it's not going to do any harm. The problem is in what this matter attracts. Dead plant matter is a breeding ground for pests and disease. Pests can hide in this plant waste, feeding off it while it is still fresh and then moving on to your plants shortly afterwards. It is a good idea to check your garden daily to clear out your dead. If this is too much work for you then at least clean out the beds whenever you go to water them, as long as you don't let any dead and rotting plant matter stick around for too long, you will most likely be okay.

Printed in Great Britain
by Amazon